YOU ARE A BELOVED CHILD OF GOD,

precious to Him in every way. He cares about you, and His faithfulness can be counted on every day. As He gives you the gift of each new morning, you have the opportunity to multiply that gift to the world.

The 365 simple suggestions in these pages present a chance to make the world a little better. The ideas may be simple *(Think about good things)* or practical *(Finish something you've already started)*. They may be inspiring Bible verses *(Love extravagantly, 1 Corinthians 13:13)* or encouraging quotes *(God is always speaking.... Listen to Him, Mother Teresa)*. Use the lines on each dated page to record blessings, reactions, prayers, or details of the day. Start any time and continue until you've filled in the whole year.

Every day is a new day with God. His love never ends. Be inspired to greet each morning with hope and courage, ready to embrace the fresh life God has for you. And let this journal help you share His love with the world.

EXPECT THE DAWN
OF A NEW BEGINNING
in the dark nights of life.

LLOYD JOHN OGILVIE

....

....

....

....

....

....

GOD BRINGS HOPE,

forgiveness, heart cleansing, peace, and power.

LUCILLE M. LAW

THE LORD WILL WORK OUT HIS PLANS FOR MY LIFE.

PSALM 138:8 NLT

START A BLESSINGS LIST.

....

....

....

....

....

....

ALLOW GOD THE PRIVILEGE OF SHAPING YOUR LIFE

...discover new depths of
purpose and meaning.

JONI EARECKSON TADA

FORGIVE
SOMEONE
whose behavior has
been hard to forgive.

....

....

....

....

....

....

YOUR LOVE, LORD, REACHES TO THE HEAVENS,

your faithfulness to the skies.

PSALM 36:5

....

....

....

....

....

....

TAKE CARE OF THE MINUTES AND THE HOURS,

and the years will take care of themselves.

START READING A BOOK

you've always meant to read.

A JOYFUL SPIRIT IS LIKE A SUNNY DAY.

It sheds a brightness over everything.

....

....

....

....

....

....

LET YOUR HEART LIVE FOREVER!

PSALM 22:26 NKJV

....

....

....

....

....

....

GOD SHALL BE MY HOPE,

my stay, my guide,
and lantern to my feet.

WILLIAM SHAKESPEARE

If I rise on the wings of the dawn,
if I settle on the far side of the sea,
**EVEN THERE YOUR
HAND WILL GUIDE ME.**

PSALM 139:9–10

GIVE GENEROUSLY.

....

....

....

....

....

....

We are the lanterns—
CHRIST IS THE LIGHT INSIDE.

OLETA SPRAY

REJOICE!

1 CHRONICLES 16:10 ESV

GOD MAKES ALL THINGS NEW. YES, EVEN YOU!

BASILEA SCHLINK

....
....
....
....
....
....

DANCE TO THE MUSIC IN YOUR HEAD.

....

....

....

....

....

SING SONGS TO THE TUNE OF HIS GLORY,

set glory to the rhythms of his praise.

PSALM 66:2 MSG

PRAY FOR
THE LEADERS
in your city, state, and nation.

....

....

....

....

....

FAITH IS TAKING THE FIRST STEP,

even when you don't see
the whole staircase.

MARTIN LUTHER KING JR.

....

....

....

....

....

....

GOD NEVER MADE ANYONE ELSE EXACTLY LIKE YOU

and He never will again.

NORMAN VINCENT PEALE

THE LORD'S FAITHFULNESS ENDURES FOREVER.

PSALM 117:2 NLT

Every day is a clean,
new page from God for us to
START AGAIN.

....

....

....

....

....

....

Each day
ENRAPTURE ME
WITH YOUR
MARVELOUS THINGS
without number.

ABRAHAM JOSHUA HESCHEL

ATTEND A CHURCH SERVICE.

COME NEAR TO GOD

and he will come near to you.

JAMES 4:8

WHAT SEEMS MUNDANE
and trivial
MAY SHOW ITSELF TO BE HOLY,
precious, part of a pattern.

LUCI SHAW

....

....

....

....

....

....

CONFRONT YOUR FEARS

and let them know
God is in control.

With lavish hand
You have spread beauty across
the world, and I know

LOVE HAS
PLANNED IT ALL.

KATHRYN BLACKBURN PECK

....

....

....

....

....

....

TRUST STEADILY
IN GOD.

1 CORINTHIANS 13:13 MSG

GOD BLESS YOU

and utterly satisfy your heart
...with Himself.

AMY CARMICHAEL

....

....

....

....

....

Remember,
IDEAS BECOME THINGS.

....

....

....

....

....

....

You, O God, are both tender and kind,
not easily angered, immense in love, and

YOU NEVER,
NEVER QUIT.

PSALM 86:15 MSG

Come and sit and

ASK HIM WHATEVER IS ON YOUR HEART.

...He has all the time in the world.

MAX LUCADO

....

....

....

....

....

....

SEND A THANK-YOU NOTE

to one of your
(current or past) teachers.

....

....

....

....

....

....

How necessary it is to
CULTIVATE
A SPIRIT OF JOY.

DOROTHY DAY

SAY "YES!"
TO MORE QUESTIONS,
experiences,
and promptings from God.

LOVE FROM
THE CENTER
OF WHO YOU ARE;

don't fake it.

ROMANS 12:9 MSG

....

....

....

....

....

....

ALL WE ARE
and all we have
IS BY THE...LOVE OF GOD!

A. W. TOZER

SING A FEW VERSES OF PSALMS ALOUD.

....

....

....

....

....

I AM LEAVING YOU WITH A GIFT

—peace of mind and heart.

JOHN 14:27 NLT

SPREAD TRUE LOVE IN THE WORLD.

MICHAEL QUOIST

SEND AN "I LOVE YOU" MESSAGE

by phone, computer,
or old-fashioned paper.

LOVE
EXTRAVAGANTLY.

1 CORINTHIANS 13:13 MSG

....

....

....

....

....

....

EVERY MORNING IS A FRESH BEGINNING.

FINISH SOMETHING
you've already started.

....

....

....

....

....

JOY IS
really a road sign
POINTING US TO GOD.

C. S. LEWIS

THE JOY OF THE LORD IS YOUR STRENGTH.

NEHEMIAH 8:10 NKJV

....

....

....

....

....

....

BUY COFFEE FOR THE NEXT PERSON IN LINE.

....

....

....

....

....

Open wide the windows
of my spirit and
**FILL ME
FULL OF LIGHT.**

CHRISTINA ROSSETTI

USE YOUR IMAGINATION

for practical things.

....

....

....

....

....

....

SING A NEW SONG TO THE LORD,

for he has done wonderful deeds.

PSALM 98:1 NLT

....

....

....

....

....

....

LIFE IS A
GLORIOUS EXPERIENCE
of discovering God's endless wonders.

WENDY MOORE

....

....

....

....

....

SLIP QUIETLY INTO
THE PRESENCE OF GOD.

....

....

....

....

....

....

SATURATE YOUR SOUL WITH THE WAYS OF JESUS.

Watch Him. Listen to Him.

JOHN PIPER

TRUST IN THE LORD WITH ALL YOUR HEART

and lean not on your own understanding.

PROVERBS 3:5

....
....
....
....
....
....

Slow down. Breathe in.
PAY ATTENTION
TO THE LITTLE THINGS.

If you are seeking after God,
you may be sure of this:

GOD IS SEEKING YOU

much more.

JOHN OF THE CROSS

TAKE THE
STAIRS TODAY.

It will give you time to pray
all the way down.

THIS IS THE DAY
THAT THE LORD HAS MADE.

PSALM 118:24 NRSV

....

....

....

....

....

....

GOD IS THE BEGINNING

—not just the starting point, but
the source of all things.

MARILYN M. MORGAN

....

....

....

....

....

....

PRAY FOR SOMEONE
YOU HAVEN'T OFFICIALLY MET.

Faith is the ability to
LET YOUR LIGHT SHINE
even after your fuse is blown.
BARBARA JOHNSON

REST SECURE IN HIM.

DEUTERONOMY 33:12

....

....

....

....

....

WELCOME EACH DAY WITH A SMILE.

·

....

....

....

....

....

....

LIVE YOUR LIFE WHILE YOU HAVE IT.

FLORENCE NIGHTINGALE

....

....

....

....

....

....

GIVE UP
ONE BAD HABIT
or at least reduce the frequency
until you have the strength to
give up the whole thing.

....

....

....

....

....

....

DON'T BE AFRAID.

...Remember the Lord, who is great and awesome.

NEHEMIAH 4:14

....

....

....

....

....

....

ALLOW YOUR DREAMS
A PLACE IN YOUR
PRAYERS AND PLANS.

Today is a great day to
SURPRISE SOMEONE
with a random act of kindness.

JOY IS THE TOUCH OF GOD'S FINGER.

PETER KREEFT

POUR OUT YOUR HEART BEFORE HIM.

PSALM 62:8 NASB

....

....

....

....

....

....

EVERY BREATH WE DRAW IS A GIFT OF HIS LOVE.

THOMAS MERTON

....

....

....

....

....

....

Take a moment during the day to
GAZE UPON THE WONDER OF GOD'S CREATION.

....

....

....

....

....

....

MARCH 16

BE STILL, AND KNOW
THAT I AM GOD.

PSALM 46:10 KJV

You've got to
DO YOUR OWN GROWING,
no matter how tall your grandfather was.

IRISH PROVERB

....

....

....

....

....

ASK, AND IT WILL BE GIVEN TO YOU.

LUKE 11:9 NKJV

Where there is hope,
ALL THINGS
ARE POSSIBLE.

TRUE GRATITUDE,
like true love,
IS SHOWN THROUGH ACTIONS,
not words.

....

....

....

....

....

....

Let today be the day
that you

TAKE A RISK FOR GOD.

....

....

....

....

....

....

In the same way I loved you,

YOU LOVE ONE ANOTHER.

JOHN 13:34 MSG

EVERY MORNING
IS A CHANCE AT A NEW DAY.

MARJORIE HINCKLEY

When you are upset,

**PRAY BEFORE
YOU SPEAK.**

....

....

....

....

....

MARCH 25

The best kind of beginning, when we are
wanting to know the will of God, is to

CONCENTRATE FIRST
ON GOD HIMSELF.

ELISABETH ELLIOT

I am the resurrection and the life.

THE ONE WHO BELIEVES IN ME WILL LIVE.

JOHN 11:25

LET GO
of things that aren't healthy for you.

DO NOT FORGET
THE JOY OF CHRIST RISEN.

MOTHER TERESA

In God's great mercy
he has caused us to
BE BORN AGAIN
INTO A LIVING HOPE,
because Jesus Christ rose from the dead.

1 PETER 1:3 NCV

MAKE A TO-DO LIST
and follow it.

The cross did what man could not do.
It granted us the right to talk with, love, and even

LIVE WITH GOD.

MAX LUCADO

....

....

....

....

....

....

LEARN TO KNOW GOD'S WILL FOR YOU,

which is good and pleasing and perfect.

ROMANS 12:2 NLT

DON'T BE AFRAID TO LAUGH OUT LOUD.

It makes people smile.

KEEP YOUR EYES ON JESUS,

who both began and finished
this race we're in.

HEBREWS 12.2 MSG

BE DELIGHTED AT THE PROSPECT OF A NEW DAY,

a fresh try, one more start,
with perhaps a bit of magic
waiting somewhere behind the morning.

JOSEPH PRIESTLEY

REFRESH YOUR SOUL

by talking to God
or reading the Bible.

....

....

....

....

....

....

YOUR DEEPEST JOY COMES WHEN... JESUS BECOMES YOUR TOTAL JOY.

A. WETHERELL JOHNSON

YOUR LOVE, LORD, REACHES TO THE HEAVENS,

your faithfulness to the skies.

PSALM 36:5

....

....

....

....

....

....

THINK ABOUT GOOD THINGS

and put your focus
on the positive side of life.

....

....

....

....

....

....

THE LORD'S GOODNESS SURROUNDS US AT EVERY MOMENT.

R. W. BARBER

SAVOR LITTLE GLIMPSES OF GOD'S GOODNESS

and His majesty, thankful for the gift of them.

I will
SING AND MAKE MUSIC
with all my soul.

PSALM 108:1

....

....

....

....

....

....

If each moment is sacred—
a time and place where we encounter God—
LIFE ITSELF IS SACRED.
JEAN M. BLOMQUIST

....

....

....

....

....

....

PRAY FOR YOUR EXTENDED FAMILY

—including the crazy aunts!

DEPEND UPON GOD'S PROMISES,

for...He will be as good as His word.

MATTHEW HENRY

Let petitions and praises
SHAPE YOUR WORRIES INTO PRAYERS.

PHILIPPIANS 4:6–7 MSG

....

....

....

....

....

....

THANK GOD FOR ALL THINGS

—hard days and lazy days, small moments
and large accomplishments,
food to eat and hands to wash the dishes.

....

....

....

....

....

....

CELEBRATE THE START OF EACH DAY WITH GOD.

WENDY MOORE

....

....

....

....

....

....

TAKE THE
FIRST STEP
on the path God
has put before you.

HOW GREAT
ARE YOUR WORKS, LORD.

PSALM 92:5

I do not ask to see the reason for it all;
I ASK ONLY TO SHARE THE WONDER OF IT ALL.

ABRAHAM JOSHUA HESCHEL

JOY...COMES FROM WITHIN.

It is a state of being.

BILLY GRAHAM

ASK AND IT WILL BE GIVEN TO YOU;

seek and you will find; knock and the
door will be opened to you.

MATTHEW 7:7

HOPE FOR
THE BEST
but, just in case,
prepare for the worst.

....

....

....

....

....

....

As for me and my house, we will
SERVE THE LORD.

JOSHUA 24:15 KJV

....

....

....

....

....

....

If you desire to be really happy, you must

MAKE GOD YOUR FINAL AND ULTIMATE GOAL.

THOMAS À KEMPIS

....

....

....

....

....

....

START A NEW HOBBY
that includes the whole family.

....

....

....

....

....

....

PUT YOUR HOPE IN GOD.

PSALM 42:5

ALWAYS BE IN A STATE OF EXPECTANCY

and see that you leave room for
God to come in as He likes.

OSWALD CHAMBERS

....

....

....

....

....

....

IT IS CHRIST WHO GIVES US LIGHT.

AUGUSTUS W. HARE

START YOUR DAY THANKING GOD FOR HIS GIFTS.

....
....
....
....
....
....

MY LIFE IS
GOD'S PRAYER.

PSALM 42:8 MSG

REJOICE DAILY.

....

....

....

....

....

....

HE MADE YOU SO YOU COULD SHARE IN HIS CREATION,

could love and laugh and know Him.

TED GRIFFEN

GRACE AND GRATITUDE
BELONG TOGETHER

like heaven and earth.

KARL BARTH

....

....

....

....

....

PRAY FOR ABSOLUTELY EVERYTHING,

ranging from small to large.

MARK 11:24 MSG

TAKE A WALK TODAY

and feel God's sunshine or mist on your face.

....

....

....

....

....

....

YOU ARE VERY SPECIAL TO GOD

as His precious child.

GARY SMALLEY AND JOHN TRENT

....

....

....

....

....

....

GUARD YOUR HEART,
for everything you do flows from it.

PROVERBS 4:23

....

....

....

....

....

....

CALL YOUR MOM
and tell her you love her.

....

....

....

....

....

....

Whether we examine the cosmos on
its largest scale or its tiniest...

GOD'S FINGERPRINTS ARE VISIBLE.

HUGH ROSS

....

....

....

....

....

SAY THANK YOU

to someone who has helped you.

....

....

....

....

....

DON'T TAKE YOURSELF TOO SERIOUSLY

—take God seriously.

MICAH 6:8 MSG

....

....

....

....

....

....

YOU ARE GOD'S CREATED BEAUTY

and the focus of His affection and delight.

JANET L. SMITH

PLANT A SEED

in a pot, a garden, or an elderly person's yard.

....

....

....

....

....

....

Today is a new day.

TODAY THERE IS
A NEW YOU

waiting to be opened to the world.

....

....

....

....

....

....

BE CONTENT
WITH WHO YOU ARE,
and don't put on airs.
God's strong hand is on you.

1 PETER 5:6 MSG

READ THE
BIBLE TODAY

and memorize one of the verses.

....

....

....

....

....

JOY COMES FROM
KNOWING GOD LOVES ME.

DR. JAMES DOBSON

....

....

....

....

....

WORSHIP GOD
IF YOU WANT THE BEST;
worship opens doors to all his goodness.

PSALM 34:9 MSG

YOUR LIFE IS
A GIFT FROM GOD,
and it is a privilege to share it with others.

MAY 21

FROM THE HEART OF GOD COMES...
THE RHYTHM OF LOVE.

KEN GIRE

KEEP ON PRAYING.

ROMANS 12:12 NLT

MAKE THE APOLOGY

you've been putting off.

....

....

....

....

....

....

With joy without and joy within,

ALL IS WELL.

JANET ERSKINE STUART

BE PRESENT IN THE MOMENT,

it is a gift of grace from God.

BE STRONG
AND COURAGEOUS.

...The LORD your God goes with you;
he will never leave you nor forsake you.

DEUTERONOMY 31:6

....

....

....

....

....

....

Success is never final.
Failure is never fatal.
IT IS COURAGE
THAT COUNTS.

THE PRESENCE OF GOD IS
a climate of strong and bracing love,
ALWAYS THERE.

JOAN ARNOLD

....

....

....

....

....

....

Clean out your closet, basement,
attic, or garage and
DONATE THE GOOD STUFF.

....

....

....

....

....

I AM WITH YOU

and will watch over you wherever you go.

GENESIS 28:15

....

....

....

....

....

....

LIVE FOR TODAY
but hold your hands open to tomorrow.

BARBARA JOHNSON

....

....

....

....

....

....

PRAY FOR THE PERSON WHO MAKES YOUR COFFEE

(even if that person is you).

....

....

....

....

....

....

LET MY HEART...
FIND PEACE IN YOU, O GOD.

AUGUSTINE

....

....

....

....

....

....

TAKE YOUR EVERYDAY, ORDINARY LIFE... AND PLACE IT BEFORE GOD

as an offering.
Embracing what God does for you is
the best thing you can do for him.

ROMANS 12:1 MSG

TRY TO MAKE SOMEONE LAUGH OUT LOUD.

....

....

....

....

....

EVERYTHING IN LIFE IS MOST FUNDAMENTALLY A GIFT.

LEO O'DONOVAN

WRITE A THANK-YOU NOTE TO GOD.

....

....

....

....

....

....

GIVE, AND IT WILL BE GIVEN TO YOU.

...The measure you give will be
the measure you get back.

LUKE 6:38 NRSV

Invite a friend to
PLAY A NEW GAME.

....

....

....

....

....

....

Stretch out your hand and

TAKE THE WORLD'S WIDE GIFT OF JOY AND BEAUTY.

CORINNE ROOSEVELT ROBINSON

TRUST YOUR FINANCIAL WORRIES,

whether you have much or little,

TO GOD.

....

....

....

....

....

....

EACH MORNING IS THE OPEN DOOR TO A NEW WORLD

—new vistas, new aims, new tryings.

LEIGH MITCHELL HODGES

Love each other with genuine affection, and

TAKE DELIGHT IN
HONORING EACH OTHER.

ROMANS 12:10 NLT

PRAY FOR YOUR PARENTS.

....

....

....

....

....

....

Take a moment to

REALLY LOOK AT
YOUR COUNTRY'S FLAG

and recall the history that it symbolizes.

HONOR YOUR
FATHER AND MOTHER.

DEUTERONOMY 5:16 NLT

START SOMETHING NEW

that you've been putting off.

....

....

....

....

....

....

GRACE...
like the Lord, the Giver,
NEVER FAILS.

JOHN NEWTON

....

....

....

....

....

....

JOY IS THE
ECSTASY OF ETERNITY

in a soul that has made peace with God.

....

....

....

....

....

GOD PROMISES TO LOVE ME ALL DAY.

PSALM 42:8 MSG

....

....

....

....

....

....

THINK OF YOUR FUTURE AND SMILE.

God isn't done with you yet!

THIS IS YOUR DAY OF SEIZING OPPORTUNITIES.

....

....

....

....

....

YOUR HEART WAS MADE FOR JOY.

Your heart was made to enjoy
the One who created it.

BE TRULY GLAD.

There is wonderful joy ahead.

1 PETER 1:6 NLT

....

....

....

....

....

....

Be there for someone.
SHOW REAL INTEREST AND CONCERN.

....

....

....

....

....

HE IS A GOD
WHO CAN BE FOUND.

A God who can be known.
A God who wants to be close to us.

STORMIE OMARTIAN

....

....

....

....

....

....

SCHEDULE FAMLY TIME
in permanent ink
on your calendars.

....

....

....

....

....

....

LOVE THE LORD YOUR GOD WITH ALL YOUR HEART

and with all your soul and with all your mind.

MATTHEW 22:37

....

....

....

....

....

YOU ARE
HANDCRAFTED BY GOD

who has a personal design and plan for you.

WENDY MOORE

....

....

....

....

....

OFFER HELP
before it is requested.

LOVE GIVES, LOVE KNOWS, AND LOVE LASTS.

JONI EARECKSON TADA

....

....

....

....

....

....

I've loved you the way my Father has loved me.

MAKE YOURSELVES AT HOME IN MY LOVE.

JOHN 15:9 MSG

....

....

....

....

....

....

GOD'S HOLY BEAUTY

comes near you, like a spiritual scent, and it

STIRS YOUR DROWSING SOUL.

JOHN OF THE CROSS

....

....

....

....

....

....

JULY 3

GO SOMEWHERE NEW
like a park or an exotic destination.

PATRIOTISM MEANS TO STAND BY YOUR COUNTRY.

THEODORE ROOSEVELT

....

....

....

....

....

I remain confident of this:

I WILL SEE THE GOODNESS
OF THE LORD

in the land of the living.

PSALM 27:13

Break clear away, once in awhile, and climb
a mountain or spend a week in the woods.

WASH YOUR SPIRIT CLEAN.

JOHN MUIR

....
....
....
....
....
....

TRY TO LIVE IN PERPETUAL WONDER.

....

....

....

....

....

....

Every morning seems to say:
THERE'S SOMETHING HAPPY ON THE WAY.

HENRY VAN DYKE

YOU HAVE MADE KNOWN TO ME THE PATHS OF LIFE.

ACTS 2:28

Don't
JUDGE EACH DAY
by the harvest you reap but
BY THE SEEDS THAT YOU PLANT.
ROBERT LOUIS STEVENSON

LET HIS LIFE BE SEEN THROUGH YOU

as a light to others.

....

....

....

....

....

....

I BELIEVE THAT GOD IS IN ME

as the sun is in the color and fragrance of a flower.

HELEN KELLER

I WILL SING OF THE MERCIES OF THE LORD FOREVER.

PSALM 89:1 NKJV

God is always speaking....
LISTEN TO HIM.

MOTHER TERESA

SIMPLIFY YOUR LIFE

by letting go of unnecessary things.

HE IS THE SOURCE OF EVERYTHING.

Strength for your day. Wisdom for your task. Comfort for your soul.

JACK HAYFORD

LIVE OPENLY
AND EXPANSIVELY!

2 CORINTHIANS 6:13 MSG

....

....

....

....

....

....

God invites *you* to
VACATION IN
HIS SPLENDOR.
...He wants to spend time with *you*.

MAX LUCADO

LIVE WITH HOPE
IN YOUR HEART

and a prayer on your tongue.

TIME IS...SO PRECIOUS

that it's only given to us moment by moment.

AMELIA BARR

BE COMPASSIONATE
AND HUMBLE.

1 PETER 3:8 NIV

LIFE IS A
SPLENDID GIFT

—there is nothing small about it.

FLORENCE NIGHTINGALE

....

....

....

....

....

....

SEND AN ENCOURAGING NOTE

to your pastor, mentor, or coach.

....

....

....

....

....

....

THE GOODNESS OF GOD IS INFINITELY WONDERFUL

more than we will ever be able to comprehend.

A. W. TOZER, ADAPTED

....

....

....

....

....

....

Don't take a single day for granted.

TAKE DELIGHT IN EACH LIGHT-FILLED HOUR.

ECCLESIASTES 11:7-8 MSG

The wonder of
the stars is enough to
RETURN ME TO
GOD'S LOVING GRACE.

MADELEINE L'ENGLE

Take a moment each day to
WRITE DOWN YOUR STORY
in a journal or letter.

....

....

....

....

....

EVERY MORNING

is a new opportunity to

BE DIPPED
AGAIN IN GOD'S GRACE.

....

....

....

....

....

LET GOD TRANSFORM YOU INTO A NEW PERSON
by changing the way you think.

ROMANS 12:2 NLT

....

....

....

....

....

....

ALL GOD'S GLORY AND BEAUTY COME FROM WITHIN,

and there He delights to dwell.

THOMAS À KEMPIS

....

....

....

....

....

....

LIGHTEN UP.

Humor is amazing medicine for your soul.

....

....

....

....

....

WE ARE ALWAYS IN THE PRESENCE OF GOD.

...There is never a non-sacred moment!

MAX LUCADO

DO GOOD
TO EVERYONE.

GALATIANS 6:10 ESV

....

....

....

....

....

....

GOD CARES ABOUT YOUR DAILY EVERYTHINGS.

KAY ARTHUR

....

....

....

....

....

That I am here is a wonderful
mystery to which I will
RESPOND WITH JOY.

....

....

....

....

....

....

GRATITUDE IS THE HEART OF CONTENTMENT.

NEIL CLARK WARREN

CAST ALL YOUR ANXIETY ON HIM

because he cares for you.

1 PETER 5:7

....

....

....

....

....

....

ALL THE WORLD IS AN UTTERANCE OF THE ALMIGHTY.

PHILLIPS BROOKS

Make a video, post a message, or
TELL A FRIEND
ABOUT GOD'S GRACE
in your life and what a blessing it is.

....

....

....

....

....

....

Person to person, moment to moment,
AS WE LOVE,
WE CHANGE THE WORLD.

SAMAHRIA LYTE KAUFMAN

THE HEAVENS PROCLAIM THE GLORY OF GOD.

The skies display his craftsmanship.

PSALM 19:1 NLT

This moment is as good as any
moment in all eternity.
RELISH THE DAY.

....

....

....

....

....

Today comes with 24 hours
of opportunities,
1,440 minutes of possibility.

MAKE THE MOST OF EACH MINUTE.

Either you
RUN THE DAY
or the day runs you.

JIM ROHN

God is love, and

WHOEVER ABIDES IN LOVE ABIDES IN GOD,

and God abides in him.

1 JOHN 4:16 ESV

....

....

....

....

....

AUGUST 15

I, not events, have the power to make
me happy or unhappy today.
I CAN CHOOSE
which it shall be.

GROUCHO MARX

KEEP IN MIND
not who you are but
WHOSE YOU ARE.

GOD DESIRES TO QUENCH YOUR DEEPEST THIRST,

to satisfy your deepest hunger.

CYNTHIA HEALD, ADAPTED

OPEN YOUR EYES AND SEE
—how good GOD is.

PSALM 34:8 MSG

THIS UNIQUE GIFT, THIS ONE DAY, CANNOT BE EXCHANGED,

replaced, or refunded. Handle with care. Make the most of it. There is only one to a customer

MAKE
the least of all that goes and
THE MOST OF ALL THAT COMES.

GIGI GRAHAM TCHIVIDJIAN

INVITE SOMEONE TO JOIN YOU

at a church service,
a Bible study, or a book club.

....

....

....

....

....

....

TAKE HEART!
I have overcome the world.

JOHN 16:33

....

....

....

....

....

....

All that is good, all that is true,
ALL THAT IS BEAUTIFUL...
COMES FROM GOD.

JOHN HENRY NEWMAN

....

....

....

....

....

....

GOD'S HAND IS ALWAYS THERE.

Once you grasp it,
you'll never want to let it go.

....

....

....

....

....

....

Joy comes when we catch the rhythms
of His heart. Peace comes when we
LIVE IN HARMONY
with those rhythms.

KEN GIRE

....

....

....

....

....

....

THE LORD GOD IS OUR SUN AND OUR SHIELD.

He gives us grace and glory.

PSALM 84:11 NLT

RECAPTURE THE POWER OF IMAGINATION

...and find that life can be full of
wonder, mystery, beauty, and joy.

SIR HAROLD SPENCER JONES

....

....

....

....

....

....

TAKE A DIFFERENT ROUTE HOME

and pray for people in the homes you pass.

....

....

....

....

....

REMEMBER YOU ARE NEEDED.

There is at least one important work to be
done that will not be done unless you do it.

CHARLES ALLEN

YOUR BEAUTY SHOULD COME FROM WITHIN YOU

—the beauty of a gentle and quiet spirit.

1 PETER 3:4 NCV

WHAT EXTRAORDINARY DELIGHT WE FIND IN THE PRESENCE OF GOD.

....

....

....

....

....

....

I LOVE THE
SWEET SMELL OF DAWN
—our unique daily opportunity to smell time—
each morning being a new beginning.

TERRI GUILLEMETS

....

....

....

....

....

....

EAT AND DRINK AND ENJOY

the fruits of [your] labor,
for these are gifts from God.

ECCLESIASTES 3:13 NLT

GOD IS GREATER than my senses,
GREATER than my thoughts,
GREATER than my heart.

HENRI J. M. NOUWEN

....

....

....

....

....

....

What you do
TODAY IS IMPORTANT
because you are exchanging a
day of your life for it.

....

....

....

....

....

....

I arise in the morning torn between a desire
to improve the world and a desire to
ENJOY THE WORLD.

E. B. WHITE

REJOICE WITH THOSE WHO REJOICE.

ROMANS 12:15 NASB

YOU DREAMERS OF THE DAY

are dangerous people, for you may

ACT ON YOUR DREAMS

with open eyes, to make them possible.

T. E. LAWRENCE, ADAPTED

....

....

....

....

....

....

He Himself gives life
and breath to everything, and
HE SATISFIES
EVERY NEED.

ACTS 17:25 NLT

WITH THE NEW DAY COMES NEW STRENGTH AND NEW THOUGHTS.

ELEANOR ROOSEVELT

....

....

....

....

....

THE LORD IS MY STRENGTH AND SHIELD.

I trust Him with all my heart.

PSALM 28:6–7 NLT

The important thing is this: to be
able at any moment to
SACRIFICE WHAT YOU ARE
FOR WHAT YOU COULD BECOME.

CHARLES DU BOS, ADAPTED

....

....

....

....

....

....

We love Him because
HE FIRST LOVED US.

1 JOHN 4:19 NKJV

Look on the new day as another
special gift from your Creator,
another golden opportunity to

COMPLETE WHAT YOU WERE UNABLE TO FINISH YESTERDAY.

OG MANDINO

JOY IS THE ECHO
OF GOD'S LIFE WITHIN US.

DRAW NEAR TO GOD

with a sincere heart and with the full
assurance that faith brings.

HEBREWS 10:22 NIV

....

....

....

....

....

When you arise in the morning, think of
WHAT A PRECIOUS PRIVILEGE IT IS TO BE ALIVE
—to breathe, to think, to enjoy, to love.

MARCUS AURELIUS

Let's not just talk about love; let's
PRACTICE REAL LOVE.

1 JOHN 3:18 MSG

You are a child of your heavenly Father.

CONFIDE IN HIM.

BASILEA SCHLINK

LET US REJOICE
AND BE GLAD IN TODAY.

PSALM 118:24, ADAPTED

....

....

....

....

....

GOD IS ALWAYS PRESENT

in the temple of your heart...His home.

....

....

....

....

....

....

Go to the library or
an educational website and
LEARN SOMETHING NEW.

What a joyful thought to realize

YOU ARE A CHOSEN VESSEL FOR GOD

—perfectly suited for His use.

JONI EARECKSON TADA

O my soul, bless GOD,
DON'T FORGET A SINGLE BLESSING!

PSALM 103:2 MSG

....

....

....

....

....

....

Take a nature walk and

PRAISE GOD FOR HIS CREATIVITY.

....

....

....

....

....

....

A LIFE TRANSFORMED
by the power of God
IS ALWAYS A MARVEL
and a miracle.

GERALDINE NICHOLAS

GOD PUTS
EACH FRESH MORNING,
each new chance of life,
INTO OUR HANDS AS A GIFT
to see what we will do with it.

SERVE HIM WITH ABSOLUTE SINGLE-HEARTEDNESS.

LUKE 4:8 MSG

Consider the awesome
reality that the
GOD
who spoke and created the universe
IS NOW SPEAKING TO YOU.

HENRY T. BLACKABY

....

....

....

....

....

GOD IS IN THE TOMORROWS.

He is there already. All the tomorrows of our life
have to pass Him before they can get to us.

EVERY DAY WE LIVE
IS A PRICELESS GIFT OF GOD,
loaded with possibilities.

DALE EVANS ROGERS

....

....

....

....

....

....

COMMIT TO THE LORD WHATEVER YOU DO,

and he will establish your plans.

PROVERBS 16:3

Let God have you, and
LET GOD LOVE YOU.
MAX LUCADO

....

....

....

....

....

SING FOR JOY

at the works of God's hands.

OCTOBER 4

EXPERIENCE GOD

in the breathless wonder and startling
beauty that is all around you.

WENDY MOORE

CLOTHE YOURSELF WITH LOVE,

which binds us all together
in perfect harmony.

COLOSSIANS 3:14, ADAPTED

OCTOBER 6

YOU ARE A
CREATION OF GOD,
UNEQUALED ANYWHERE
in the universe.

NORMAN VINCENT PEALE

PRAISE GOD

from whom all blessings flow.

TO PRAY IS TO CHANGE.

This is a great grace.

RICHARD J. FOSTER

FOLLOW GOD'S EXAMPLE

...as dearly loved children

EPHESIANS 5:1

....

....

....

....

....

....

OCTOBER 10

YOU CAN MAKE THIS DAY
—each moment of this day—
**A MOMENT OF
HEAVEN ON EARTH.**

TRY SEEING PEOPLE THROUGH GOD'S EYES.

WORSHIP IS...WONDER, AWE, AND GRATITUDE

for the worthiness, the greatness,
and the goodness of our Lord.

NANCY LEIGH DEMOSS

BE WHAT
YOU WERE MADE TO BE.

ROMANS 12:6, ADAPTED

....

....

....

....

....

Yesterday is dead,
tomorrow hasn't arrived yet.
I have just one day, today, and

I'M GOING TO BE HAPPY

in it.

GROUCHO MARX

What good news!

GOD KNOWS ME COMPLETELY AND STILL LOVES ME.

....

....

....

....

....

....

Be still, and in the quiet moments,

LISTEN TO THE VOICE
OF YOUR HEAVENLY FATHER.

His words can renew your spirit.

JANET L. SMITH

....

....

....

....

....

GOD IS ALL
MERCY AND GRACE

—not quick to anger, is rich in love.

PSALM 145:8 MSG

BECOMING A CONTENTED PERSON IS A PROCESS,

never an instant decision.

CHARLES R. SWINDOLL

THIS DAY
is all that is good and fair.
IT IS TOO DEAR,
with its hopes and invitations,
**TO WASTE A MOMENT
ON YESTERDAYS.**

RALPH WALDO EMERSON

He knows the rhythm of my spirit
and knows my heart thoughts.
GOD IS AS CLOSE
AS BREATHING.

....

....

....

....

....

....

EVERY GOOD AND PERFECT GIFT IS FROM ABOVE,

coming down from the Father
of the heavenly lights.

JAMES 1:17

....

....

....

....

....

....

We are never more fulfilled than when
OUR LONGING FOR GOD
IS MET BY HIS PRESENCE
in our lives.

BILLY GRAHAM

....

....

....

....

....

....

DONATE YOUR TIME,

money, talent, or blood.

....

....

....

....

....

....

JOY IS
not the absence of trouble, but
THE PRESENCE OF CHRIST.

WILLIAM VANDERHOVEN

....

....

....

....

....

OCTOBER 25

LOVE GOD...
WALK IN HIS WAYS

...so that you will live, really live,
live exuberantly, blessed by GOD.

DEUTERONOMY 30:16 MSG

OCTOBER 26

The measure in which we
should love Him is to

LOVE HIM
WITHOUT MEASURE.

BERNARD OF CLAIRVAUX

....

....

....

....

....

....

BEGIN YOUR DAY
BY TALKING WITH GOD.

We have been in God's thought from
all eternity, and in His creative love,

HIS ATTENTION
NEVER LEAVES US.

MICHAEL QUOIST

HOLD ON FOR
DEAR LIFE TO GOOD.

ROMANS 12:9 MSG

WE COME THIS MORNING— LIKE EMPTY PITCHERS TO A FULL FOUNTAIN.

...O Lord—open up a window of heaven....
And listen this morning.

JAMES WELDON JOHNSON

OCTOBER 31

It is better to give one shekel a
thousand different times
than a thousand shekels at once, because
**EACH TIME YOU GIVE,
YOU BECOME A KINDER PERSON.**

....

....

....

....

....

There are only two ways to live your life. One is as though nothing is a miracle. The other is as though

EVERYTHING IS A MIRACLE.

RICHARD CRASHAW

....

....

....

....

....

....

CREATE IN ME A CLEAN HEART, O GOD;

and renew a steadfast spirit within me.

PSALM 51:10 NKJV

SERVICE IS THE RENT
WE EACH PAY FOR LIVING.

It is not something to do in your spare
time; it is the very purpose of life.

MARIAN WRIGHT EDELMAN

One vote can change a nation,
One life can make a difference.
THAT DIFFERENCE
STARTS WITH YOU.

....

....

....

....

....

....

BE ASSURED,

if you walk with Him and look to Him
and expect help from Him,

HE WILL NEVER FAIL YOU.

GEORGE MUELLER

....

....

....

....

....

....

NOVEMBER 6

TAKE DELIGHT
IN THE LORD
and he will give you
the desires of your heart.

PSALM 37:4

IT IS ONLY WITH GRATITUDE THAT LIFE BECOMES RICH.

DIETRICH BONHOEFFER

SHARE YOUR DREAMS

with a friend.

....

....

....

....

....

....

BE AN INSTRUMENT OF GOD'S PEACE.

ST. FRANCIS OF ASSISI, ADAPTED

....

....

....

....

....

....

IT'S IN CHRIST THAT WE FIND OUT WHO WE ARE

and what we are living for.

EPHESIANS 1:11 MSG

FAITH AND HOPE ARE
nothing if they are not
RENEWED EVERY MORNING.

....

....

....

....

....

....

KEEP YOUR INBORN SENSE OF WONDER.

God's love...is a beautiful,
eternal gift, held out to us in the hands
of love. All we have to do is

SAY "YES!"

JOHN S. J. POWELL

SURELY YOUR GOODNESS AND LOVE WILL FOLLOW ME

all the days of my life.

PSALM 23:6

....

....

....

....

....

....

PRAY WITH SOMEONE

who is going through a tough time.

In the morning let our hearts
gaze upon God's love...
and in the beauty of that vision, let us

GO FORTH TO MEET THE DAY.

ROY LESSIN

Take the time to
THANK A
PUBLIC SERVANT
for a daily service that is
often taken for granted.

SEEK THE LORD YOUR GOD

[and] you will find him.

DEUTERONOMY 4:29

....

....

....

....

....

....

MAKE YOUR LOVE VISIBLE

through little acts of kindness, shared activities,
words of praise and thanks, and
willingness to get along.

EDWARD E. FORD

NOVEMBER 20

HUG YOUR CHILD

—or sister or mom—with real gusto today.

START A
gratitude, Scripture, or
PRAYER JOURNAL.

....

....

....

....

....

....

GIVE THANKS TO THE LORD,

for he is good!
His faithful love endures forever.

PSALM 136:1 NLT

TODAY IS THE BEGINNING OF A WONDERFUL FUTURE.

GRATITUDE UNLOCKS THE FULLNESS OF LIFE.

It turns what we have into enough, and more.

MELODY BEATTIE

BE FILLED WITH JOY,

always thanking the Father.

COLOSSIANS 1:11–12 NLT

GROW AS BEAUTIFUL
AS GOD MEANT YOU TO BE

when He thought of you first.

GEORGE MACDONALD

CLIMB THAT MOUNTAIN,

whatever it is for you,
and stand triumphantly at the top.

The ability to

SHARE SOMEONE'S GRIEF

is a gift from God.

JANETTE OKE

BLESS THE LORD,
O MY SOUL:

and all that is within me,
bless his holy name.

PSALM 103:1 KJV

Less is more.
GOD IS IN THE DETAILS.

MIES VAN DER ROHE

....
....
....
....
....

GIVE TO SOMEONE WHO CANNOT PAY YOU BACK.

LISTENING TO GOD IS A FIRSTHAND EXPERIENCE.

MAX LUCADO

SEE HOW GREAT HE IS

—infinite, greater than anything you
could ever imagine or figure out!

JOB 36:26 MSG

....

....

....

....

....

....

SEND A
FAMILY PHOTO
to family far away
and ask for one in return.

....

....

....

....

....

....

GOD HAS GIVEN YOU SOMETHING TO DO

in the future that no one else can do.

RUTH SENTER, ADAPTED

GIVING IS THE SECRET OF A HEALTHY LIFE

...not necessarily money, but whatever you have of encouragement and sympathy and understanding.

....

....

....

....

....

....

ALWAYS BE EAGER TO PRACTICE HOSPITALITY.

ROMANS 12:13 NLT

This is the true joy of life, to
BE USED UP FOR A PURPOSE
recognized by yourself as a mighty one.

GEORGE BERNARD SHAW, ADAPTED

....

....

....

....

....

....

Today is a great day to
BE A VOLUNTEER.

....

....

....

....

....

TRUST
FEARLESSLY.

....
....
....
....
....
....

CELEBRATE GOD ALL DAY, EVERY DAY.

I mean, *revel* in him!

PHILIPPIANS 4:4 MSG

LET GOD'S PEACE INFUSE EVERY PART OF TODAY.

WENDY MOORE

....

....

....

....

....

....

SHOW PATIENCE
AND COMPASSION

to those who are not showing it to you.

....

....

....

....

....

....

LET CHRISTMAS IN ITS DEEPEST MAGIC POSSESS YOUR MIND.

The Lord of Glory, "endless, eternal and unchangeable in His being, wisdom, power, and holiness," became...a *baby*.

JACK HAYFORD

BELIEVE IN HIM

and rejoice with joy that is inexpressible.

1 PETER 1:8 ESV

GOD LOVES YOU
IN THE MORNING SUN

and the evening rain, without caution or regret.

BRENNAN MANNING

GREAT IS THE LORD,

and greatly to be praised.

1 CHRONICLES 16:25 ESV

The "air" which our souls need also envelops
all of us at all times and on all sides.

GOD IS ROUND ABOUT US.

OLE HALLESBY

YOU WILL FILL ME WITH JOY IN YOUR PRESENCE.

ACTS 2:28

CHRISTMAS IS THE CELEBRATION OF

the keeping of a promise....

A SAVING PROMISE.

MICHAEL CARD

....

....

....

....

....

....

REJOICE! CELEBRATE ALL THE GOOD THINGS

that GOD, your God, has given
you and your family.

DEUTERONOMY 26:10-11 MSG

LOVE'S THE THING.

The rest is tinsel.

PAM BROWN

....

....

....

....

....

....

Slow down, pay attention, and
EXPERIENCE THE WONDER OF THE SEASON.

....

....

....

....

....

....

CHRISTMAS...
IS LOVE IN ACTION.

DALE EVANS ROGERS

THE SAVIOR

—yes, the Messiah, the Lord—

HAS BEEN BORN TODAY

in Bethlehem, the city of David!

LUKE 2:11 NLT

DEAR LORD...
SHINE THROUGH ME,

and be so in me that every soul
I come in contact with may feel
Your presence in my soul.

JOHN HENRY NEWMAN

....

....

....

....

....

....

DECEMBER 27

TAKE TIME TO
COUNT THE BLESSINGS
OF THE SEASON.

OUR HOPE
IS IN THE LORD.

PSALM 33:20 NCV

....
....
....
....
....
....

Grasp the fact that
GOD IS FOR YOU.

J. I. PACKER

TRUST THE PAST
TO THE MERCY OF GOD,

the present to His love, and the
future to His providence.

AUGUSTINE

....

....

....

....

....

....

Do not dwell on the past. See,

I AM DOING A NEW THING!

ISAIAH 43:18-19

....

....

....

....

....

....

Ellie Claire™ Gift & Paper Corp.
Minneapolis, MN 55378
EllieClaire.com

New Every Morning A 365-Day Journal
© 2013 Ellie Claire Gift & Paper Corp.
ISBN 978-1-60936-912-5

The forms of LORD and GOD in quotations from the Bible represent the Hebrew *Yahweh*,
while Lord and God represent *Adonai*, in accordance with the Bible version used.

Compiled by Marilyn Jansen
Cover and interior design by ThinkPen | thinkpen.com
Typesetting by Jeff Jansen | aestheticsoup.net

Printed in China